Wouldn't you like to create your very own cartoons?
In *Cartoon Fun* Don Conroy gives the essential techniques.
Follow the basic guidelines and very soon you will be on the way to drawing everything from birds to dinosaurs, cats to ladybirds, and monsters galore.

This definitive book has been published in response to the enormous demand from teachers and young people all over the country who watch Don every week on *The Den* and have learned so much from him over the years.

First published 1993 by The O'Brien Press Ltd.,
20 Victoria Road, Dublin 6, Ireland.

All rights reserved. No part of this book may be reproduced
or utilised in any form or by any means, electronic or
mechanical, including photocopying, recording, or by any
information storage and retrieval system without permission
in writing from the publisher. This book may not be
sold as a remainder or bargain book without permission
in writing from the publisher.

Copyright © Don Conroy
British Library Cataloguing-in-publication Data
A catalogue reference for this title is available
from the British Library.

10 9 8 7 6 5 4 3 2

ISBN 0 – 86278 – 358 – 5

The O'Brien Press receives assistance from
The Art Council/An Chomhairle Ealaíon

Typesetting and layout: Cathy Henderson
Illustration and cover design: Don Conroy
Colour separations: Lithoset, Dublin
Printing: Guernsey Press, Guernsey, Channel Islands

Other books by well-known artist and writer Don Conroy include:

Wings Series:
On Silent Wings
Wild Wings
Sky Wings

Tales of Woodlore Series:
The Owl Who Couldn't Hoot
The Tiger Who Was a Roaring Success
The Bat Who Was All in a Flap
The Hedgehog's Prickly Problem

The Celestial Child

CARTOON FUN
with Don Conroy

The O'Brien Press
Dublin

To my family and friends

Contents

Introduction	6	Cats	49
Head to Toe	7	Lion's Head	50
Head Construction	8	Fox	51
Head Shapes	10	Hippo and Dogs	52
Eyes	12	Mouse and Hedgehog	54
Noses	13	Rabbit and Badger	55
Expressive Hands	14	Dolphin and Whale	56
Human Feet	16	Animals' and Birds' Feet	57
Expressive Faces	17	Animation	58
Young Heads	18	Reptiles	59
People	19	Shark, Octopus and Crab	62
Baby	22	Worms, Ladybirds and Flies	63
Action Lines	23	**Dinosaurs**	64
Body Language	26	**Making Things**	70
Clowns	28	**Trees**	74
Action Figures	30	**Christmas**	75
Posture	32	Christmas Owl	76
Singer	33	**Scary Things**	78
Movement – Gnomes	34	Egyptian Mummy	80
Birds Galore	35	Frankenstein's Monster	82
Sparky	36	Dracula	84
Duck	38	Ghosts	86
Barn Owl	40	**Comic Strips**	87
Long-eared Owl	42	Dialogue Balloons	89
Animals Galore	44	**Superheroes**	90
Elephant	45	Action Figures	91
Puppy Dog	46	**Don's Friends**	92
Hedgehog	47	**Caricatures**	94

INTRODUCTION

This book is designed to give you the complete instructions you will need to draw fun cartoons.

Most of us associate cartoons with something that looks funny. However, the word cartoon originally meant 'finished drawing'. Leonardo da Vinci's most exquisite drawing of 'The Virgin on the Rocks' is a beautiful example. Usually the word 'cartoon' would be seen alongside the title.

Cartoons as we know them have been around for a long time. In the 18th century, artists began drawing satirical cartoons to make famous people look funny or foolish. Kings, queens, princes, lords, were fair game for the cartoon artists, but politicians were the main targets.

Cartoonists today are still doing this political cartooning, which is usually featured in newspapers and magazines.

The 19th century saw the beginning of both the comic strip and the cartoon strip and things really began to take off in the early part of the 20th century. Cartoon characters such as Popeye, Superman, Batman, became world-famous, delighting and entertaining millions of children and adults all over the world. Cartoon strips led to comic books, as well as to animated movies such as *Snow White and The Seven Dwarfs*, *Dumbo*, *The Jungle Book* and the short cartoons featuring Mickey Mouse or Tom and Jerry.

In recent times, art critics and collectors alike are becoming increasingly aware of the artistic and monetary value of the under-rated art form we call cartooning.

The ancient Chinese had a saying, 'you cannot call yourself an artist until you make a thousand mistakes', so don't worry if you make a mess; you can learn from mistakes.

Don't trace!

Start on what comes most easily to you. This will give you confidence to tackle the tougher drawings later.

The main thing is to enjoy yourself. You can have hours of fun learning to draw cartoons. Later on you can try making your own cartoons. Who knows – maybe one of your cartoons could be as famous as Bart Simpson or Snoopy!

HEAD TO TOE

FACES

Let's begin by drawing simple faces.
First draw a rough circle as below.
The vertical line defines the middle of the face.
The horizontal line is the eyeline.

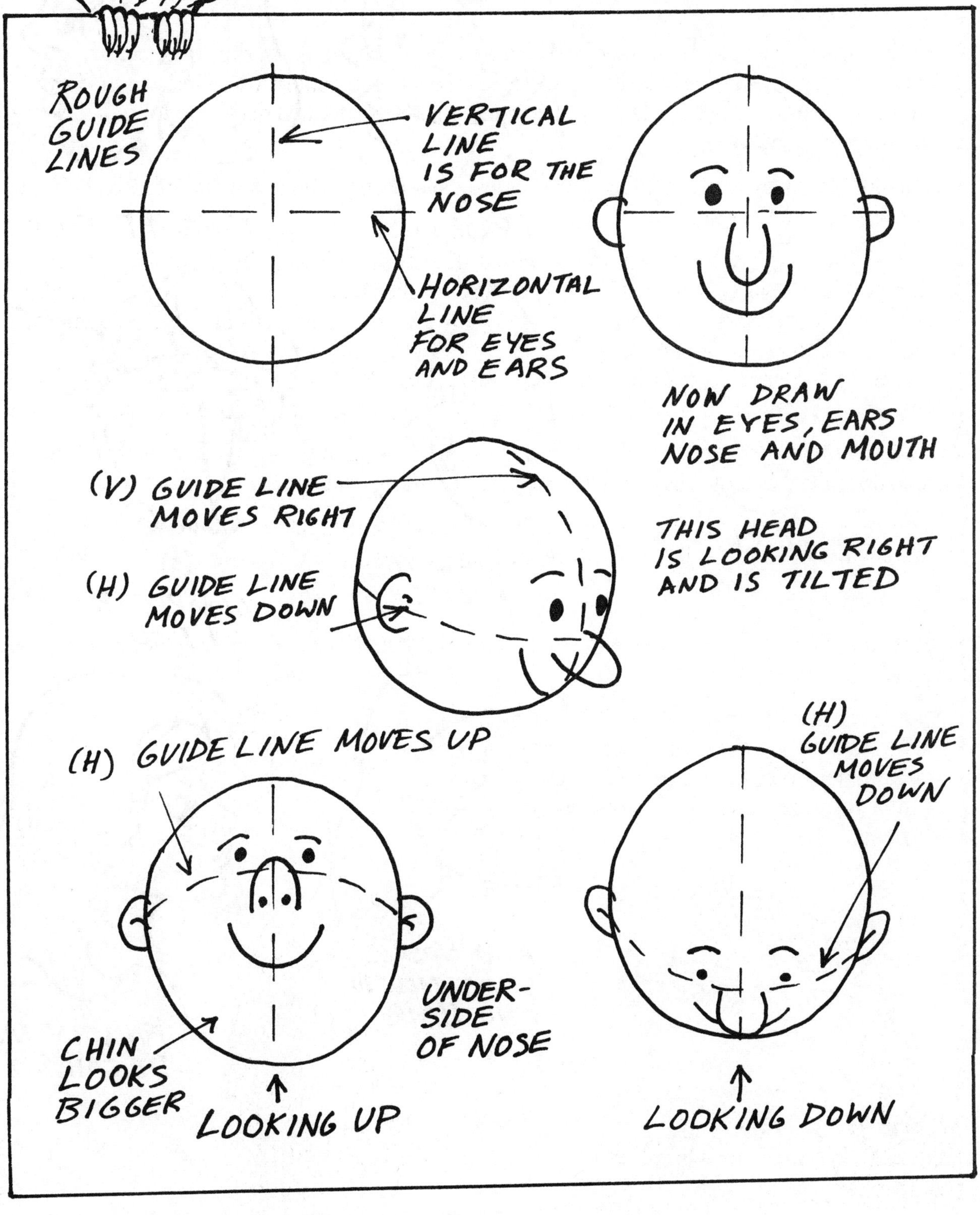

ROUGH GUIDE LINES

VERTICAL LINE IS FOR THE NOSE

HORIZONTAL LINE FOR EYES AND EARS

NOW DRAW IN EYES, EARS NOSE AND MOUTH

(V) GUIDE LINE MOVES RIGHT

(H) GUIDE LINE MOVES DOWN

THIS HEAD IS LOOKING RIGHT AND IS TILTED

(H) GUIDE LINE MOVES UP

CHIN LOOKS BIGGER

UNDER-SIDE OF NOSE

↑ LOOKING UP

(H) GUIDE LINE MOVES DOWN

↑ LOOKING DOWN

7

HEAD CONSTRUCTION (female)

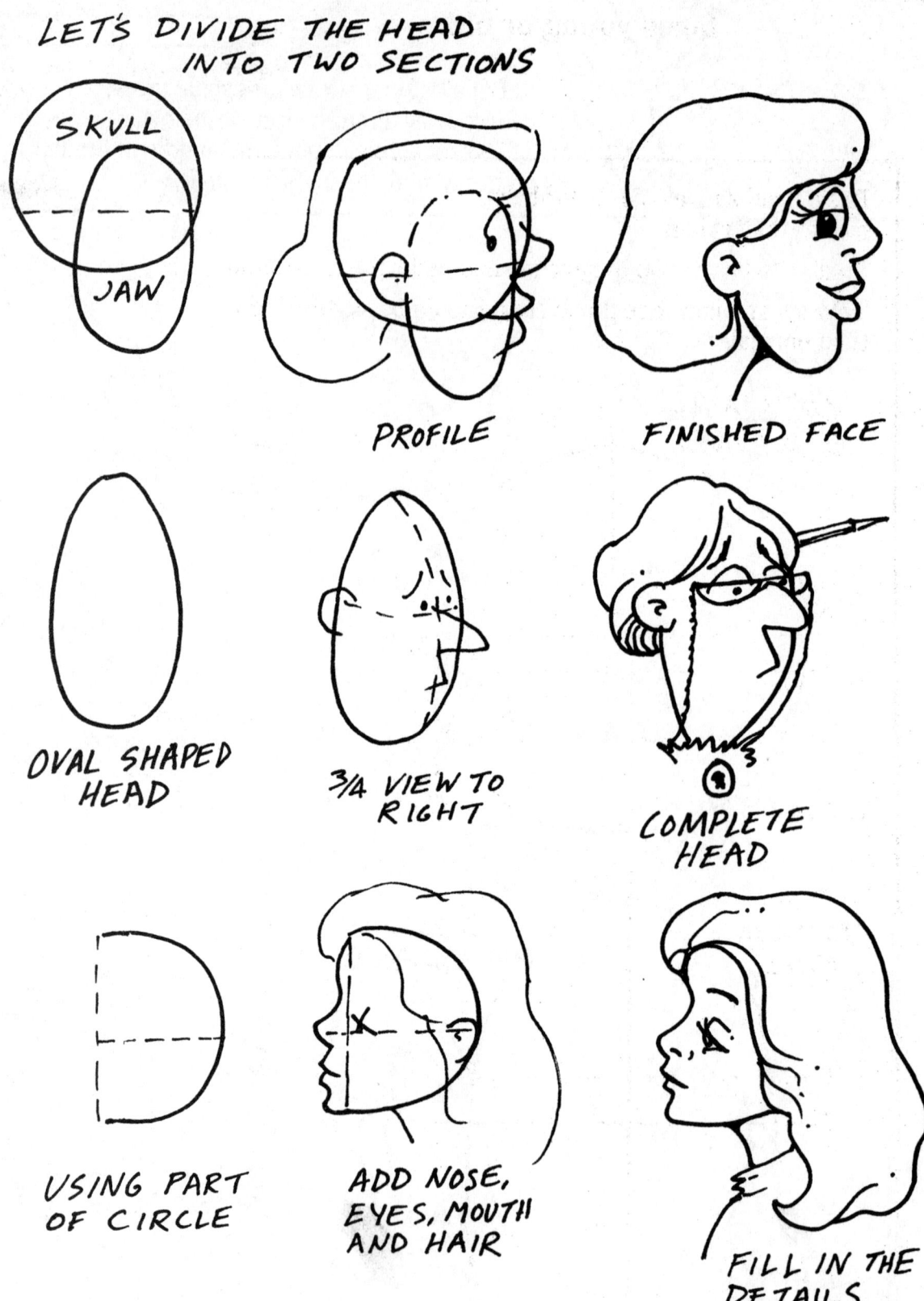

Try using circles and ovals.
The results can be very interesting.

A few simple hints for drawing faces young or old.

Basic head shape – circle for baby, oval for older man.

To draw a baby drop the eyeline and make the face rounder.

To draw an older face the eyeline should be slightly higher than normal.

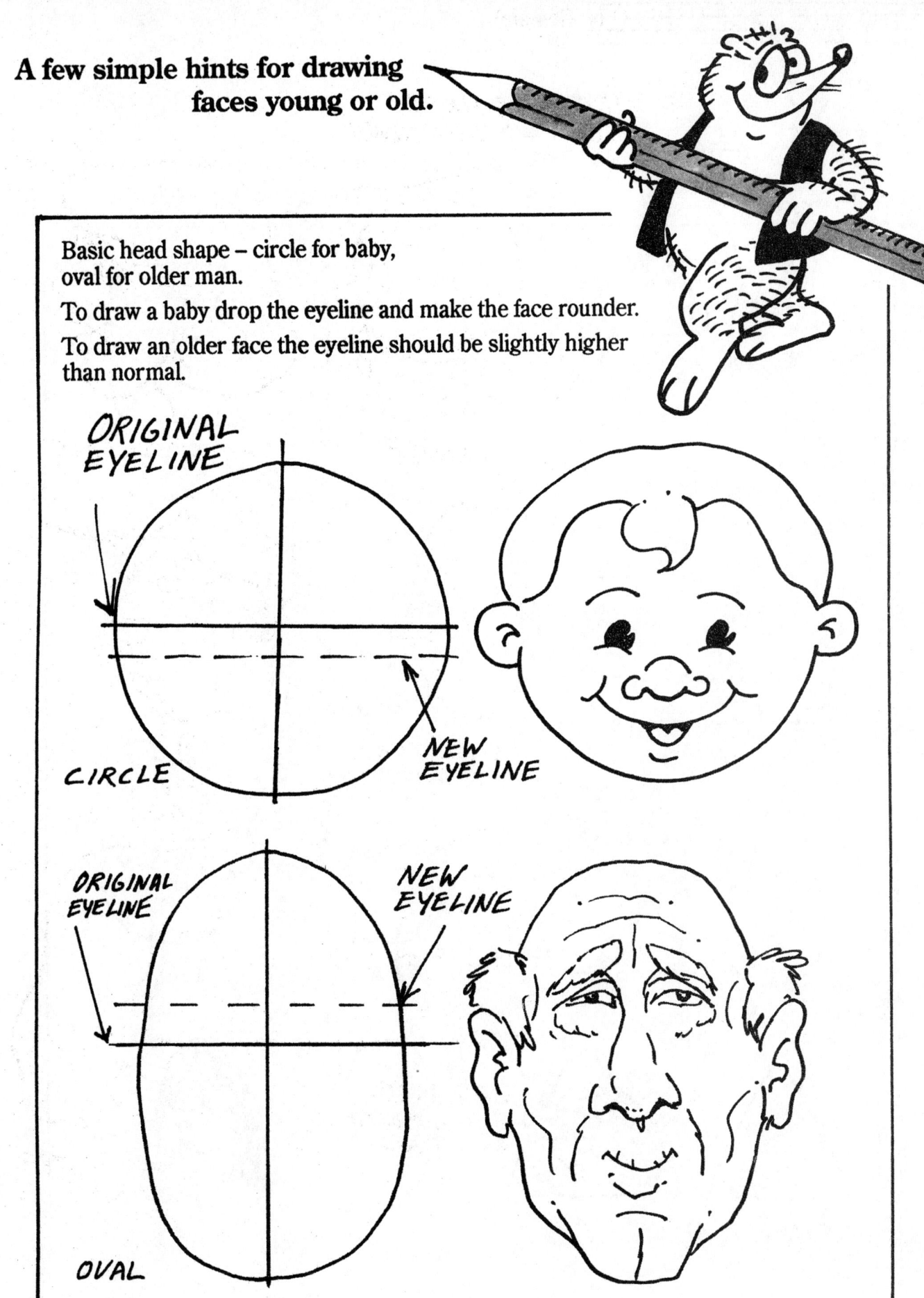

HEAD SHAPES

THIS IS TO GIVE YOU A HEAD START

By using these different shapes you can come up with some very unusual faces and expressions.

EGG

SQUARE

WEDGE

OVAL

PEANUT

PEAR

TRIANGULAR

JELLY-BEAN

EYES

GET AN EYEFUL OF THIS

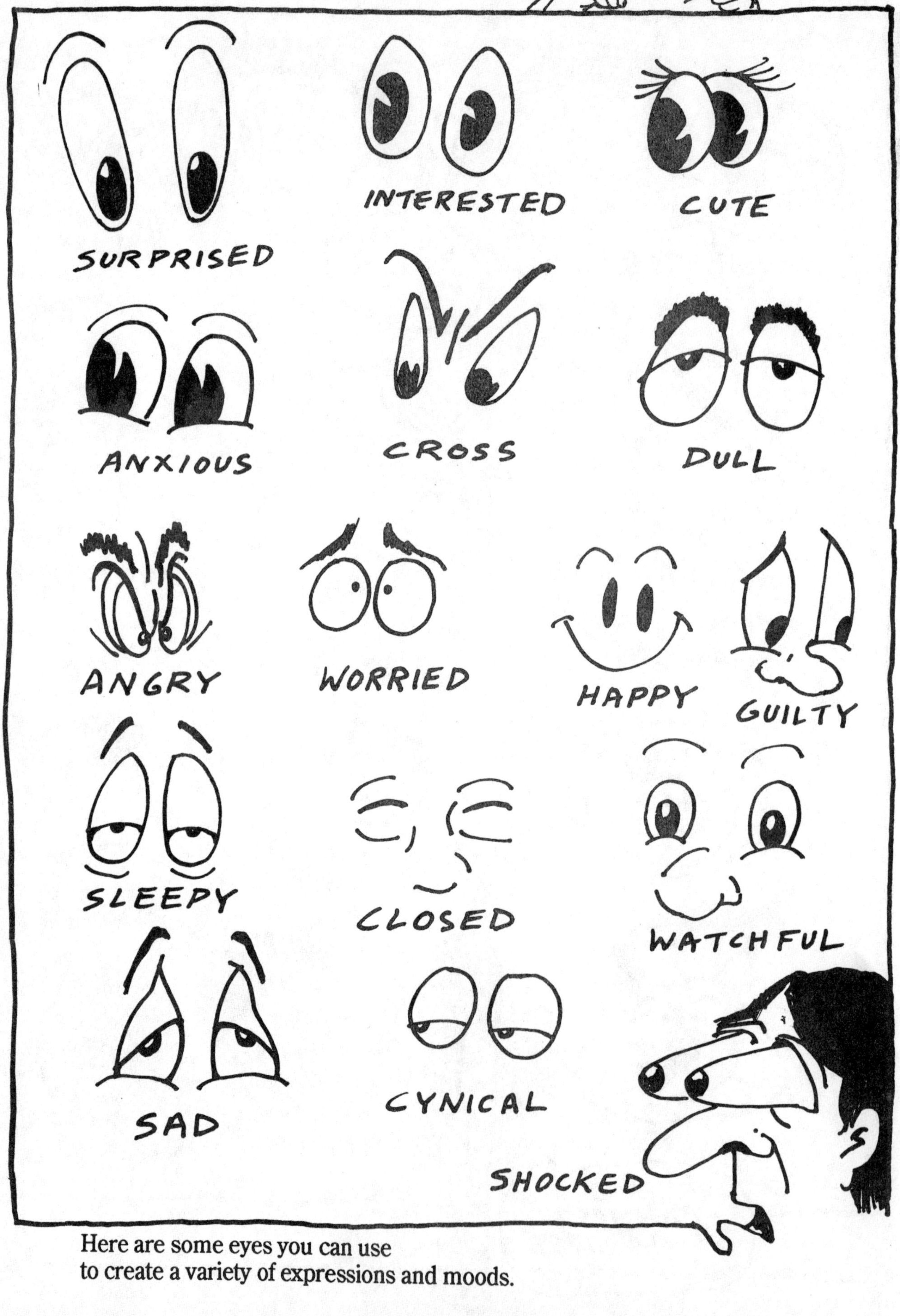

SURPRISED INTERESTED CUTE

ANXIOUS CROSS DULL

ANGRY WORRIED HAPPY GUILTY

SLEEPY CLOSED WATCHFUL

SAD CYNICAL SHOCKED

Here are some eyes you can use to create a variety of expressions and moods.

Noses can come in all shapes and sizes.
Beaky, drooping, sloping, puggy…
They can tell a lot about character.

NOSES

EXPRESSIVE HANDS

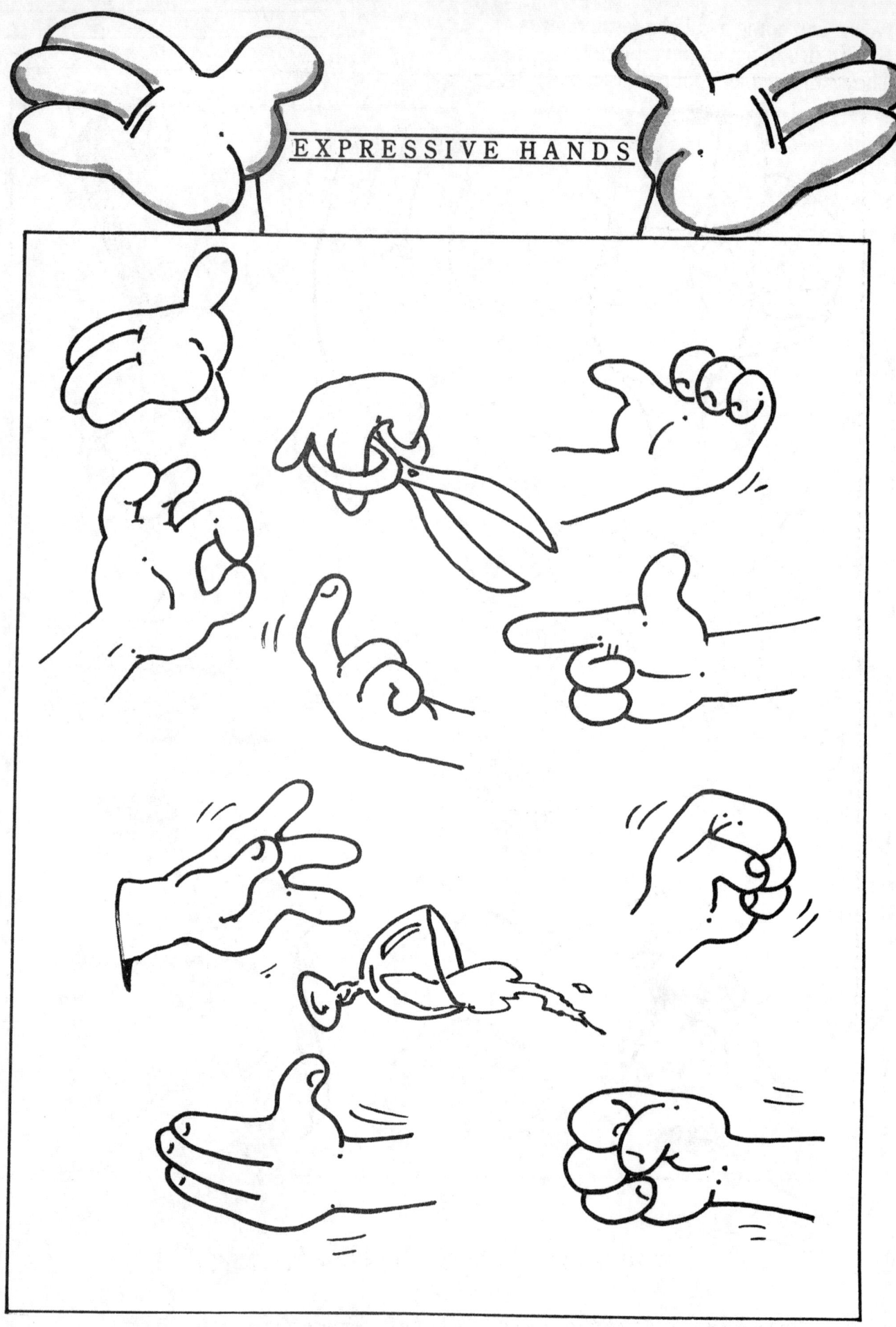

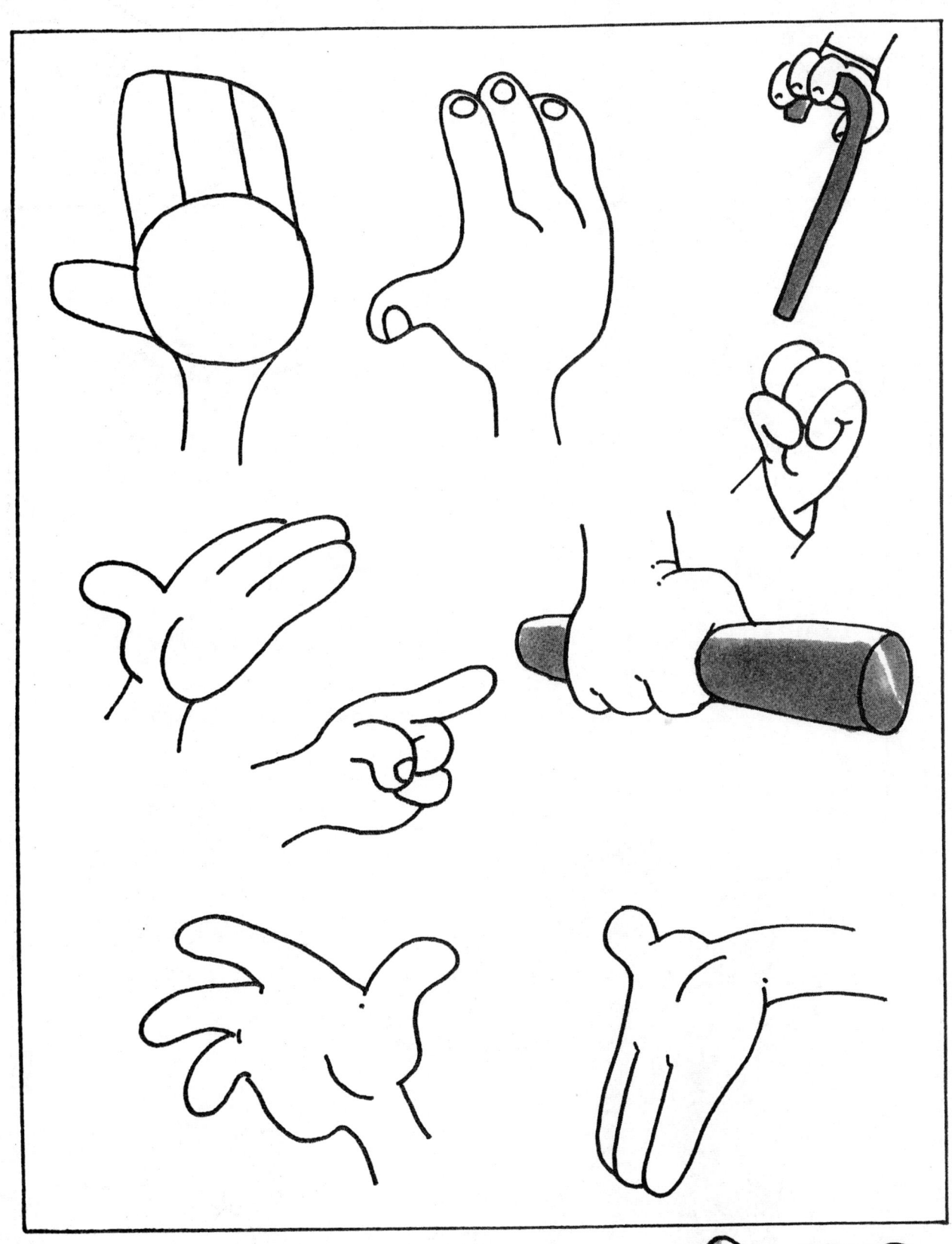

How to draw expressive hands.

Remember cartoon hands usually have three fingers and a thumb. Take a look at famous cartoon characters and you will see the three-finger and thumb hand is standard.

HUMAN FEET

Like the cartoon hand,
the cartoon foot usually has four toes, not five.
It's important to match the feet
with the rest of the character's body.

EXPRESSIVE FACES

Have a go at copying these faces, then try some of your own.

YOUNG HEADS

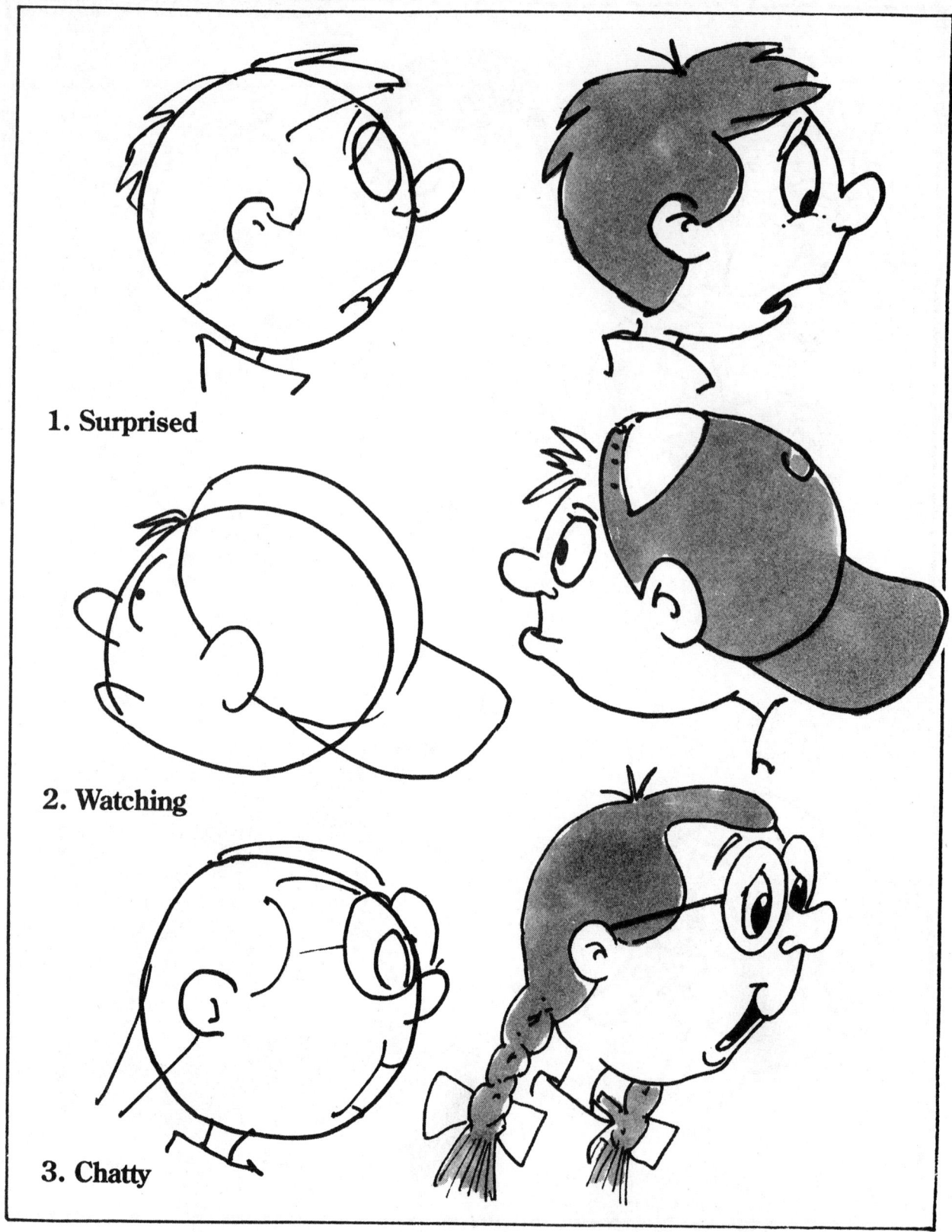

1. Surprised
2. Watching
3. Chatty

Little noses, big eyes, huge round heads

PEOPLE

A cartoon is more than just a head. As with faces, try to get expression and movement into the body. Start using these egg shapes to build up the figure.

The average head fits into the human body seven times.
In a cartoon it's usually reduced to four times.

The torso is the focal point of the body, not the arms and legs.

BABY

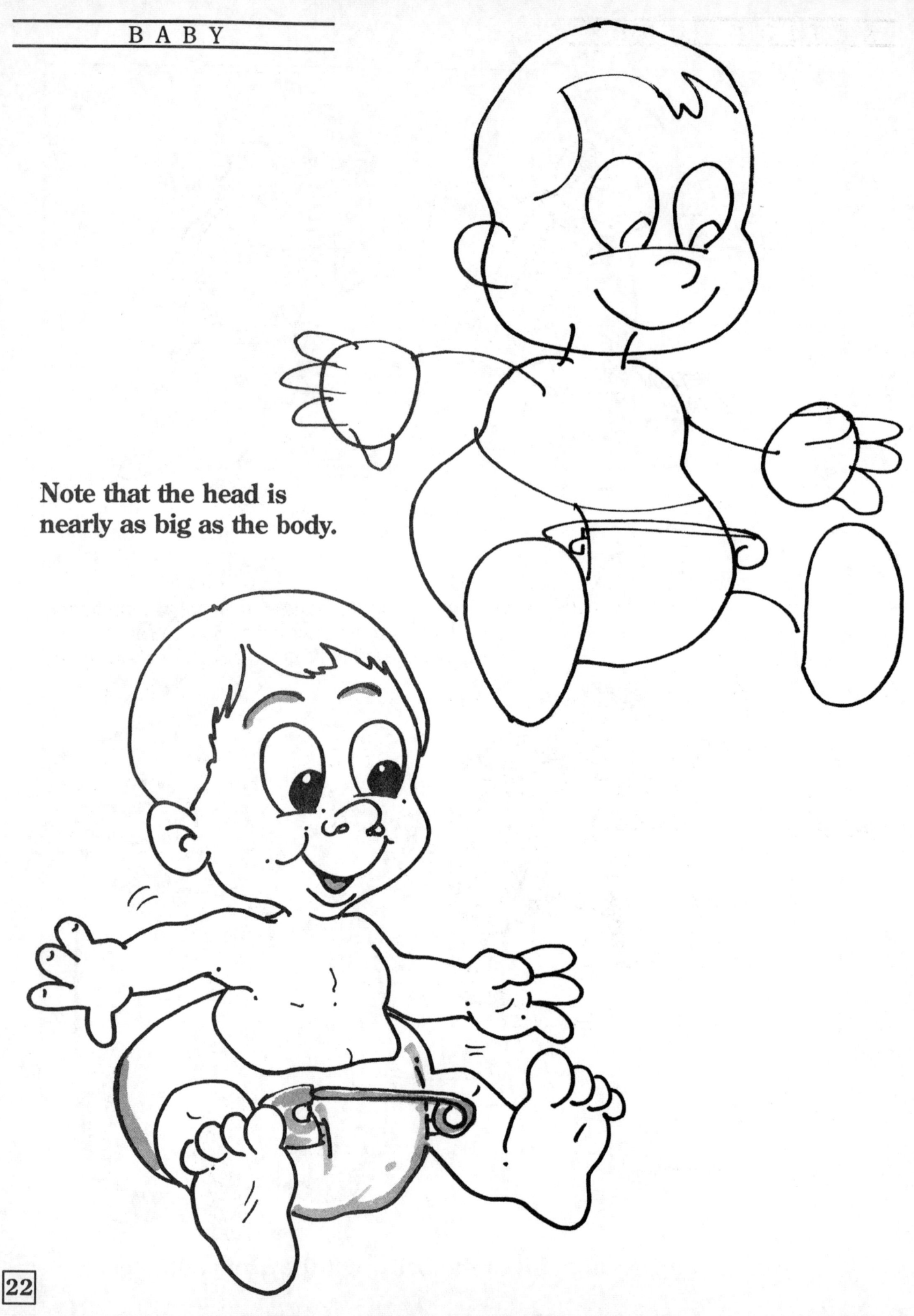

Note that the head is nearly as big as the body.

ACTION LINES

The body bends and twists in motion (the limbs moving in all directions). This can be achieved by using an action line. The action line follows the natural curve of the spine.

ACTION LINES

These little lines beside the body give it a sense of movement.

BODY LANGUAGE

Body gestures can suggest thoughts and feelings.

The hands raised by the conductor as he is beginning to conduct.

The other figure is showing expectation and determination – fists clenched, tongue anticipating meal.

CLOWNS

Realistic cartoon.
Long arms, wide body, legs tapered.
Note hands have correct number of fingers.

ACTION FIGURES

Language of the body.

30

POSTURE

YOUNG MAN

Try experimenting with these simple forms to build your own figures.
Note the pronounced movement and tilted body.

PROPHET

OLDER MAN RESTING

SINGER

Extravagant character – short, stubby with a round head and large body and mouth.
Short arms and legs. Big feet.

MOVEMENT - GNOMES

This is a good way to get a feeling of movement.

BIG HEAD
LONG ARMS
SHORT LEGS

Remember to think of the body as being 'flexible' and able to move in almost any direction.

BIRDS GALORE

SPARKY

Hi! I'm Sparky.
You will get a chance to draw me later.

First draw an egg-shaped head.
Then you can build on different beaks
(or bills, as birders call them).

DUCK

How to construct the head and body.

Try for expression and movement.

Puzzled bird (eyes telling the story). Has mistaken a shoelace for a worm.

BARN OWL

Barny Owl

You can use the same basic techniques to draw a realistic owl. This is a typical pose of a barn owl sitting on a post.

Illustration from the novel
On Silent Wings by Don Conroy.

LONG-EARED OWL

Big eyes, upright body and small beak.

Owl in flight – ear tufts lie flat on head so they are not seen.

42

You are looking at star quality here, so make sure you draw me properly. Okay?

ANIMALS GALORE

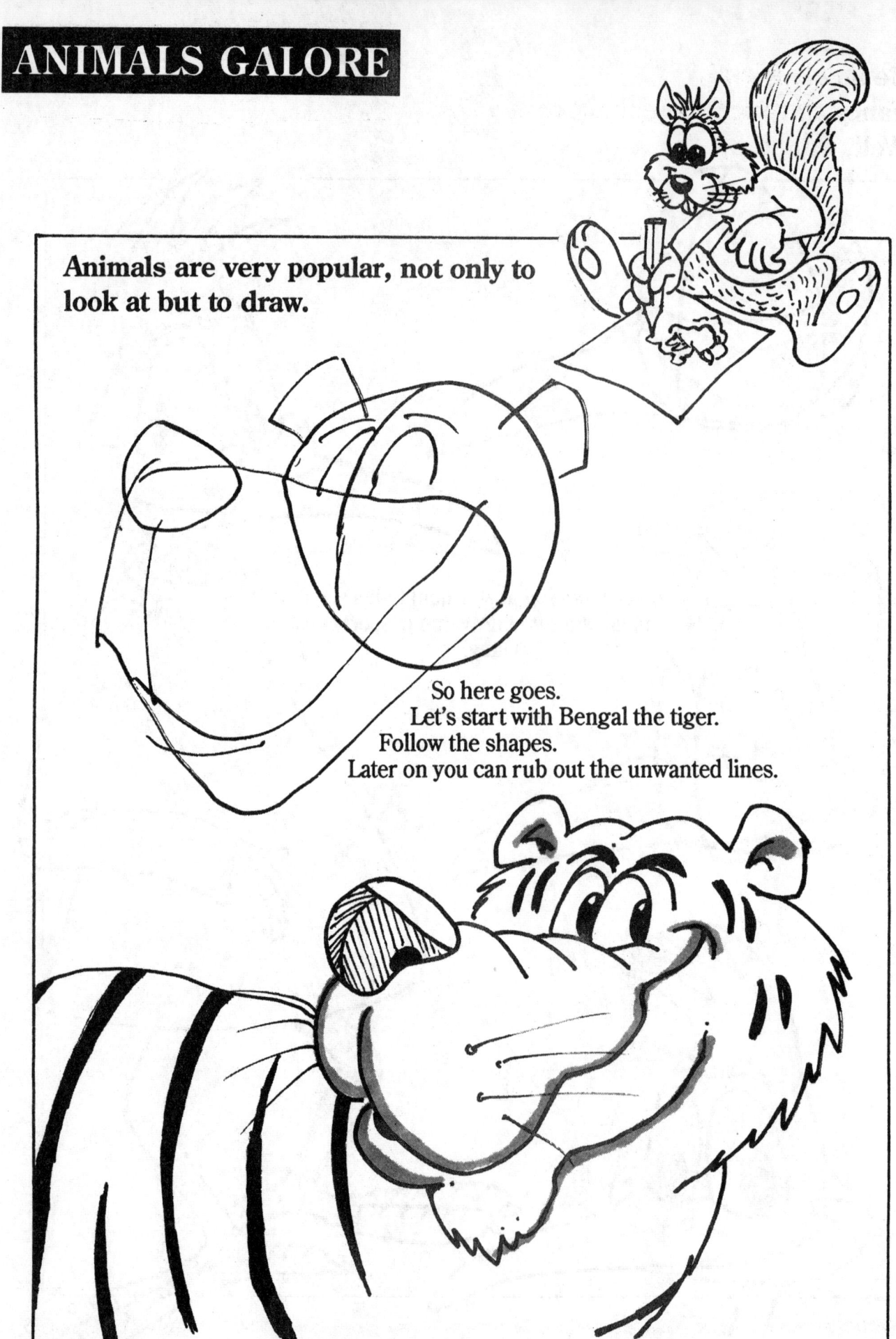

Animals are very popular, not only to look at but to draw.

So here goes.
Let's start with Bengal the tiger.
Follow the shapes.
Later on you can rub out the unwanted lines.

ELEPHANT

**Be an ele-friend.
Fancy starting an elephant with a circle!
Well, why not?**

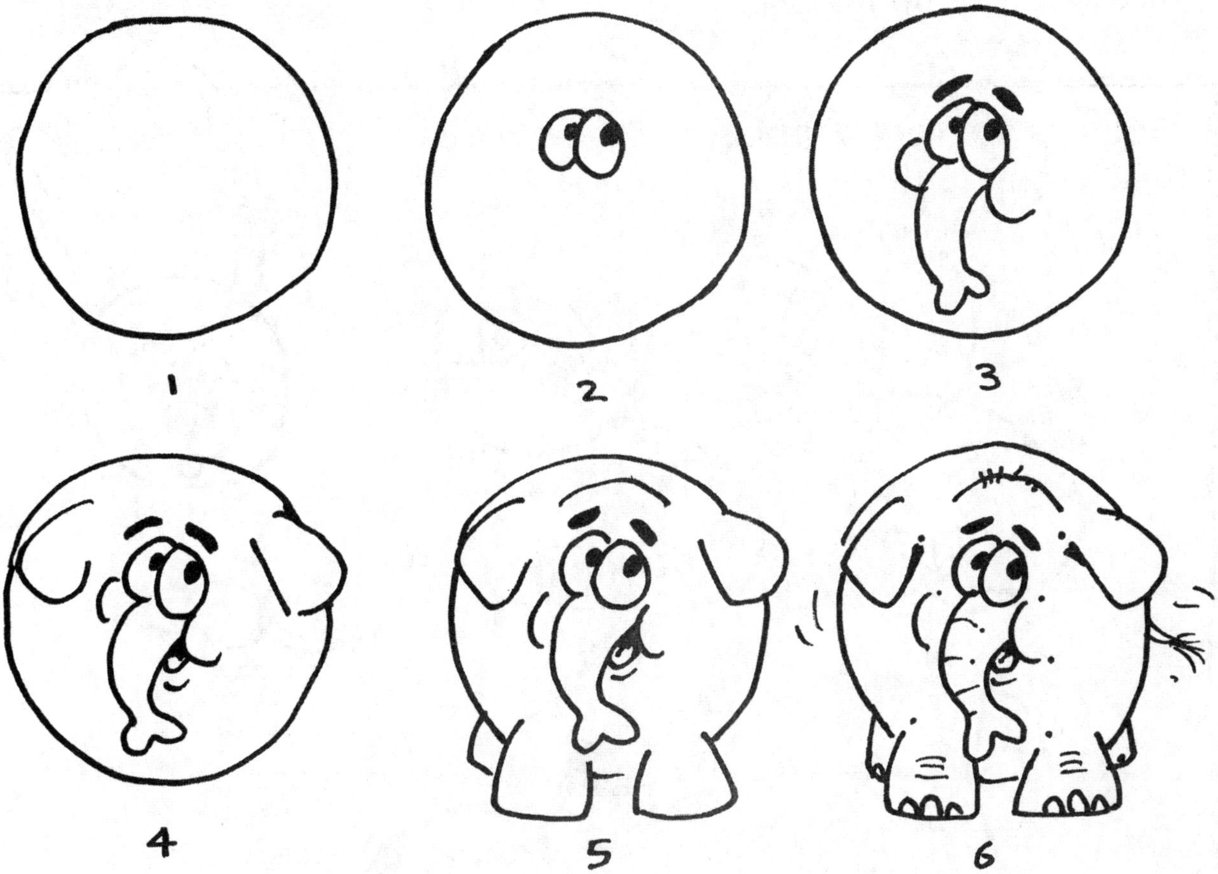

HOW TO DRAW AN ELEPHANT

Take it step by step.
Draw a rough circle as above.
Follow the progression of drawings to complete the elephant.

45

PUPPY DOG

Here is a cute puppy dog.

Take your time and don't worry if you make a mistake.
Remember what the ancient Chinese painter said:
'You can't say you're an artist until you make a
thousand mistakes.'

HEDGEHOG

Harry sitting among the flowers.

47

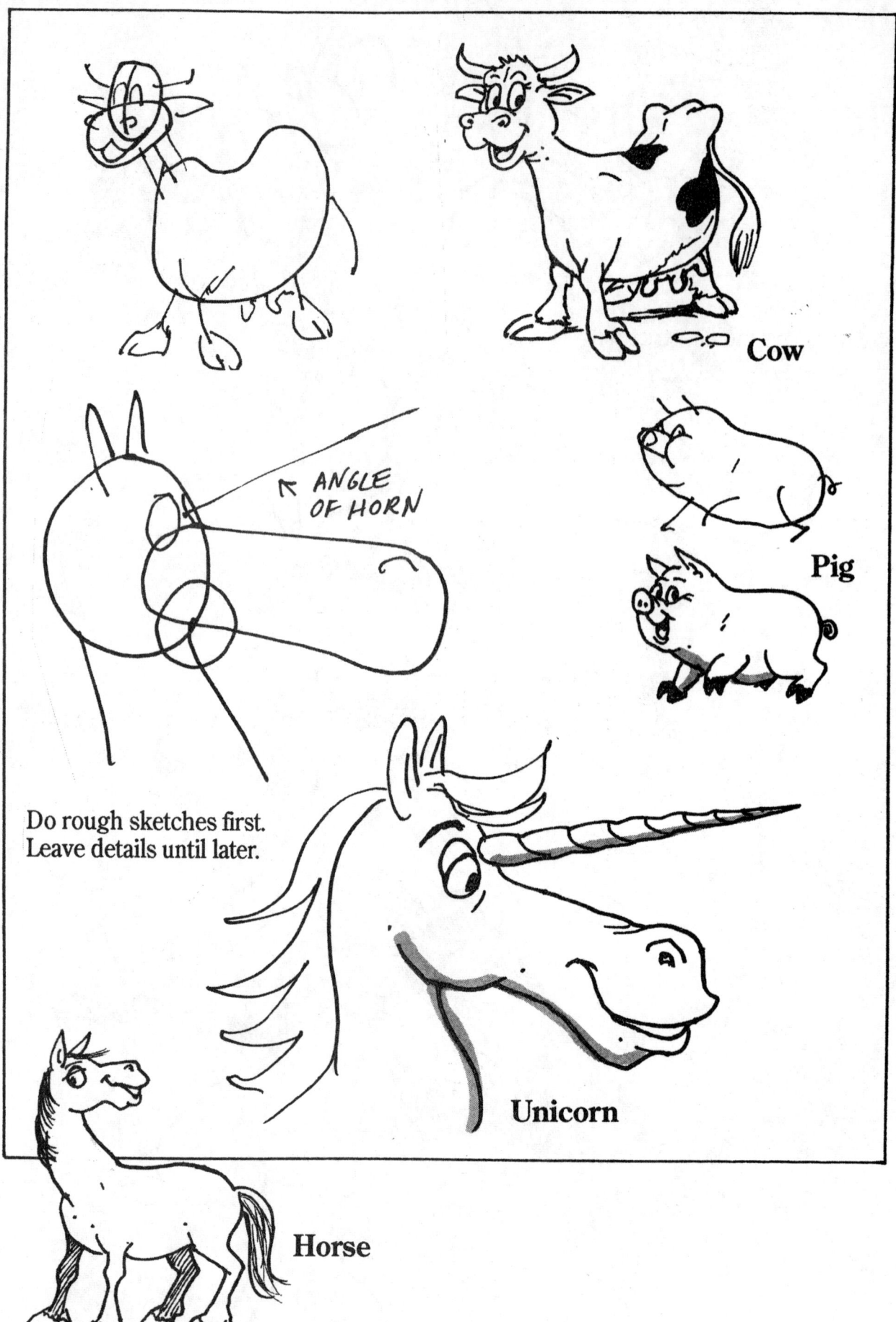

CATS

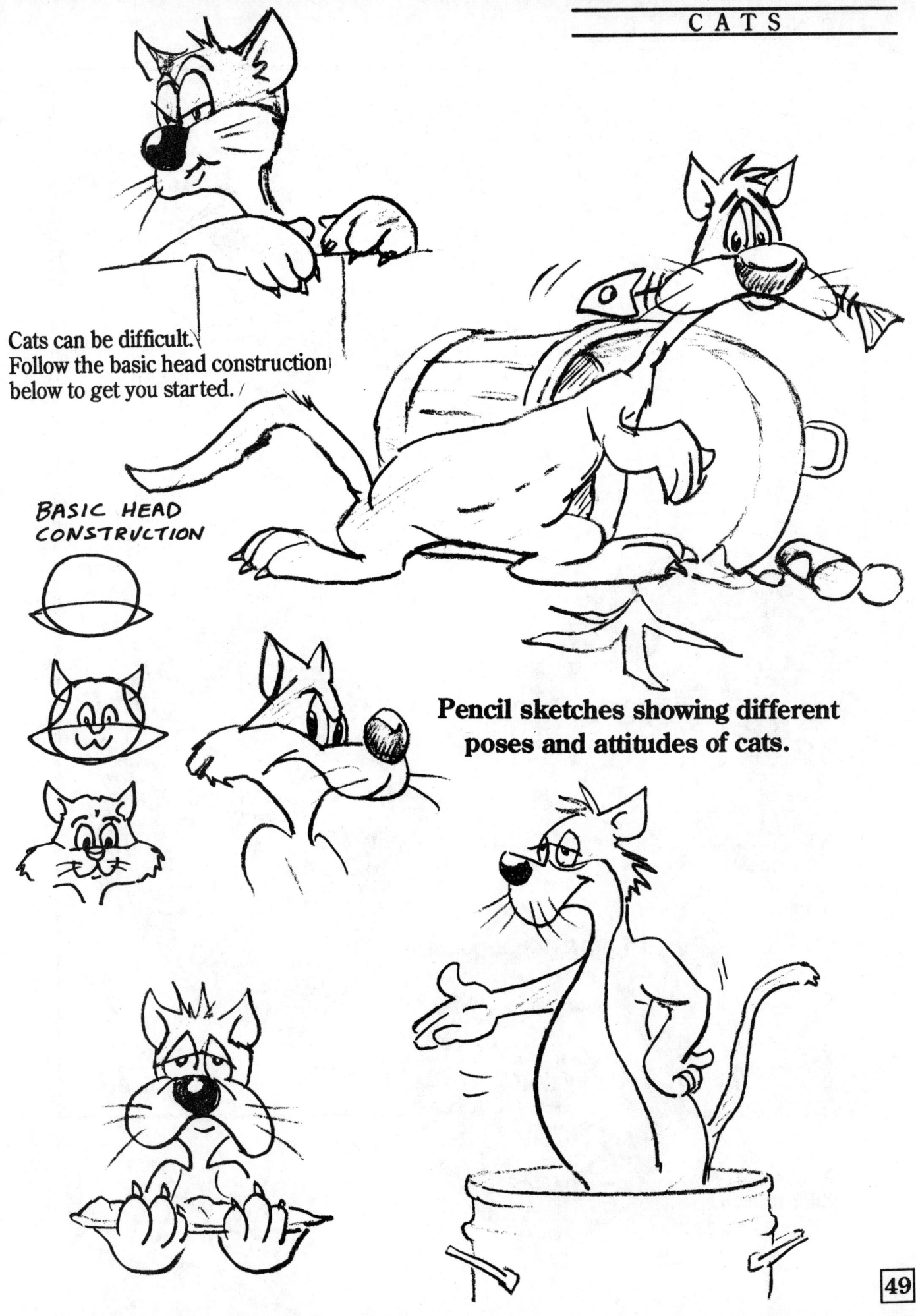

Cats can be difficult. Follow the basic head construction below to get you started.

BASIC HEAD CONSTRUCTION

Pencil sketches showing different poses and attitudes of cats.

LION'S HEAD

RELAXED

Male lion has the mane.

ANNOYED

I'M RELATED HONEST!

ANGRY

CONTENTED

These were drawn with a thin and a thick felt-tipped marker.

WHAT AM I DOING ON THIS PAGE?

This is what a fox normally looks like before we cartoonists get our hands on it.

FOX

Fox appears rather worried now that the fox hunting season has begun. By putting an animal in an upright position we humanise it.

WE ARE NOT AMUSED

HIPPO & DOGS

Hippo has bumpy head, elephant-like feet. Suggest folds of fat on body.

Guard dog has square head and sharp features.

Running dog has round back and short stubby head.
Black nose.
Body of dog goes from curve to curve, giving him a very round appearance.

Watching

Sleeping

Barking

Various types of dog in different poses.

MOUSE & HEDGEHOG

Alert mouse. Eyes and mouth show he has seen something tasty to eat.

Hedgehog thinking. Hand under chin helps to create the effect.

RABBIT & BADGER

Here are two kinds of cartoon rabbit.

Ears are always prominent.
Body is more pear-shaped in the fat rabbit.
Body of other rabbit is long and skinny.

Bently Badger in motion.
Head is set forward.
Pointed head and large frame.

55

DOLPHIN & WHALE

Dolphins seem very joyful creatures.
Here is one leaping in the air.
Body has a banana shape.

The whale is a massive creature.
Here it is just below the water.
Body is tapered like a tube.

ANIMALS' & BIRDS' FEET

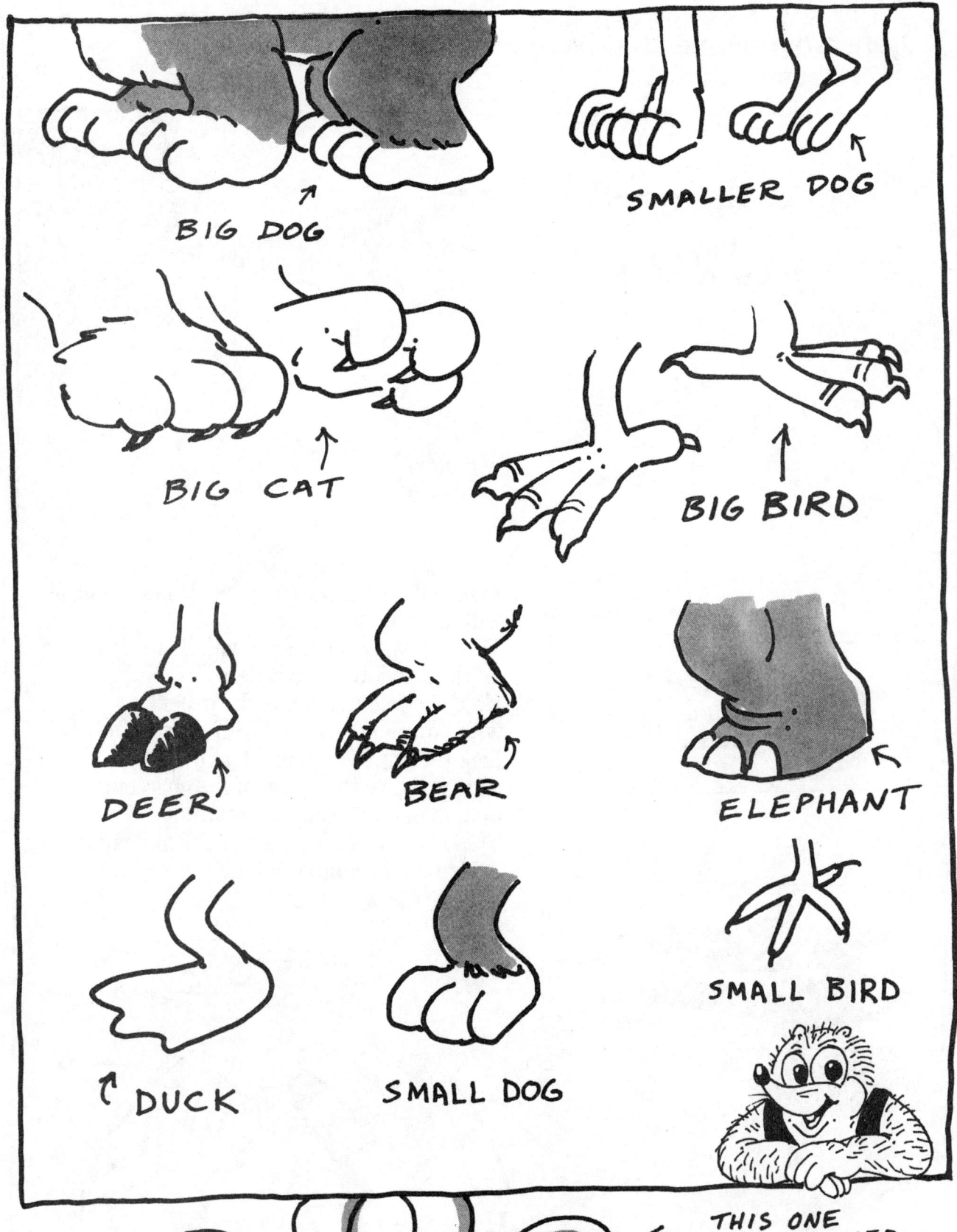

57

ANIMATION

Here are a couple of ideas to animate a head.

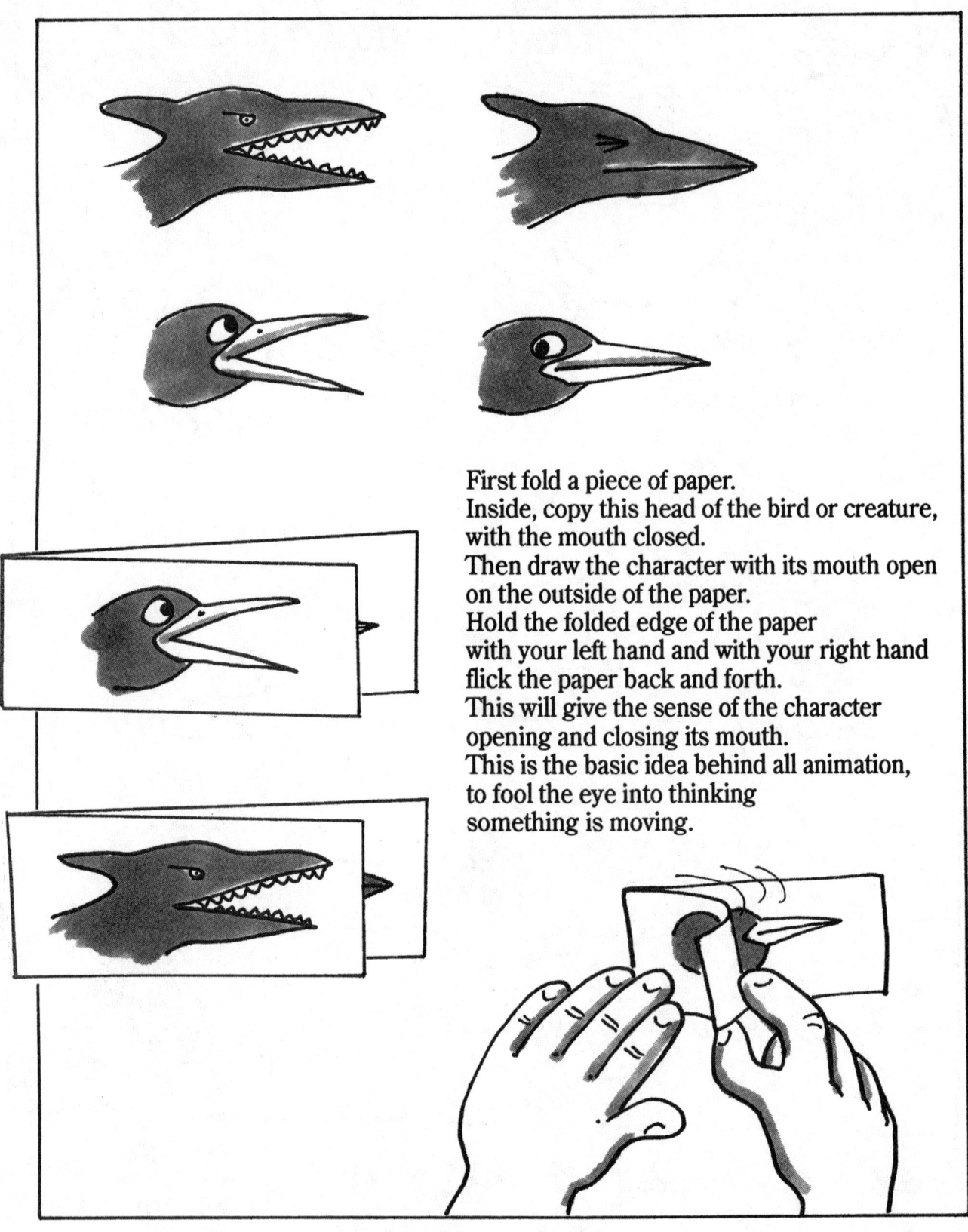

First fold a piece of paper.
Inside, copy this head of the bird or creature, with the mouth closed.
Then draw the character with its mouth open on the outside of the paper.
Hold the folded edge of the paper with your left hand and with your right hand flick the paper back and forth.
This will give the sense of the character opening and closing its mouth.
This is the basic idea behind all animation, to fool the eye into thinking something is moving.

REPTILES

Here is a jolly turtle.

Note the large head and eyes, tiny lower jaw.
Head like the beak of a parrot.

Crocodile

Broad head, wide mouth, snout is tapered.

Long back and tail, with small feet.

Snake

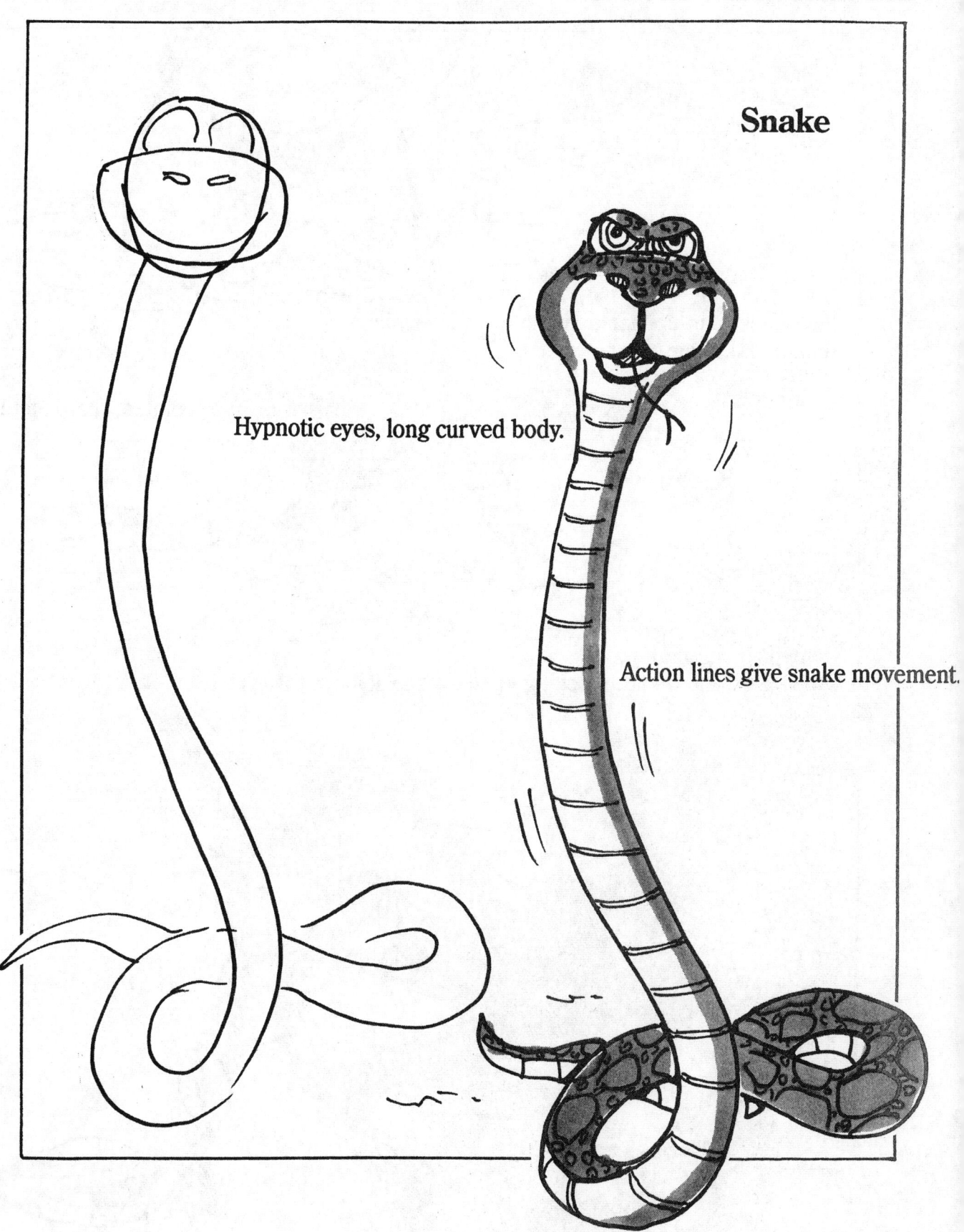

Hypnotic eyes, long curved body.

Action lines give snake movement.

SHARK, OCTOPUS & CRAB

'Jaws' pose, but upturned mouth gives it a smile, making it less aggressive looking.

Sharp fins, nose pointed, sharp teeth.

Octopus looks grumpy.
Cross eyes, and mouth reaching up to eyes to achieve the effect.

Crab ready to do battle.
Eyes suggest rest of body is hidden, which of course it is not.

WORMS, LADYBIRDS & FLIES

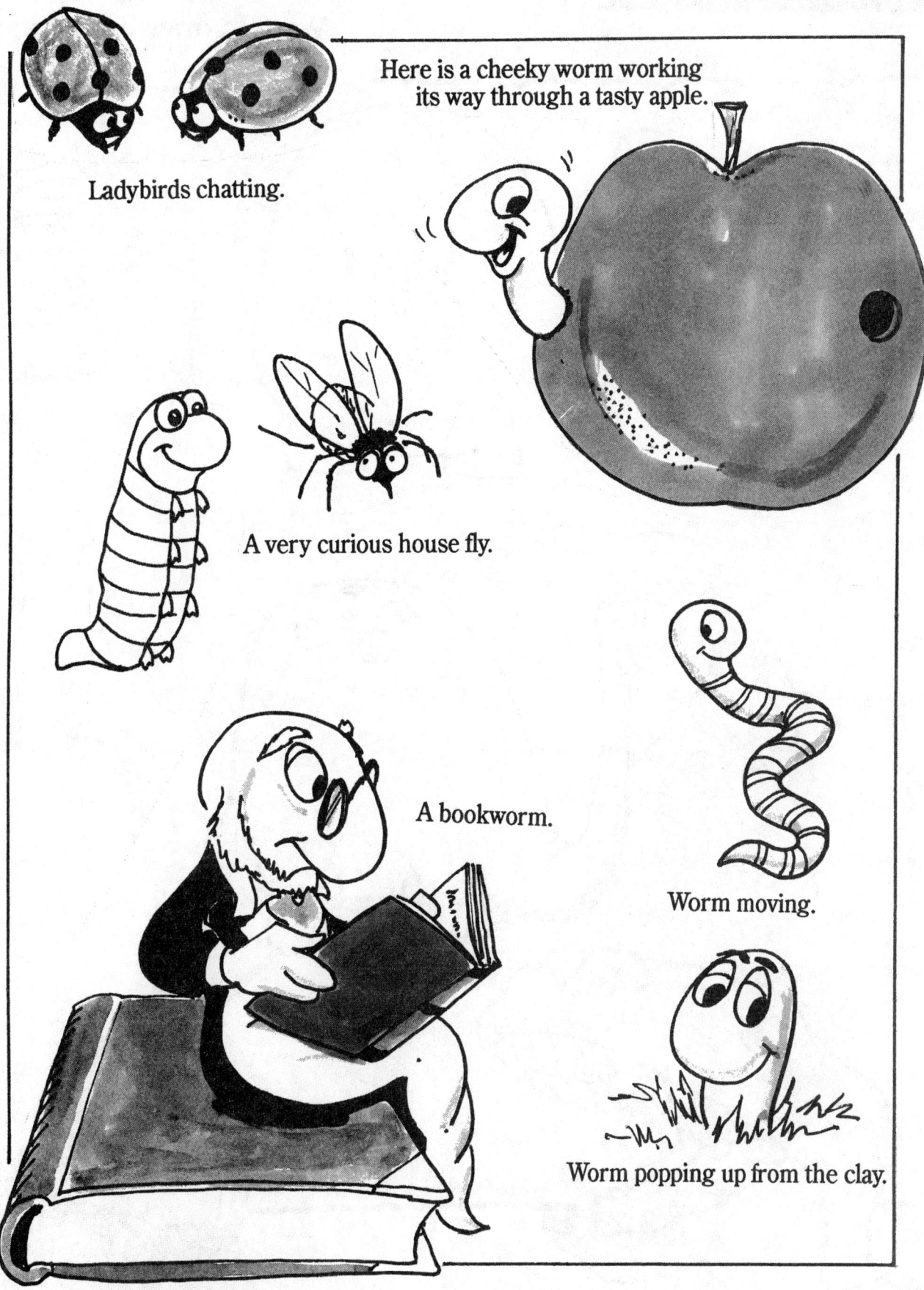

Ladybirds chatting.

Here is a cheeky worm working its way through a tasty apple.

A very curious house fly.

A bookworm.

Worm moving.

Worm popping up from the clay.

DINOSAURS

Want to draw dinosaurs?

Stegosaurus measured up to 6 metres (about 20 feet).
Spiky-backed dinosaur of the Jurassic period.

Tyrannosaurus Rex
– probably the best known dinosaur.
Its name means King Tyrant Lizard.
It was about 6 metres tall (20 feet).
A powerful flesh-eating beast.

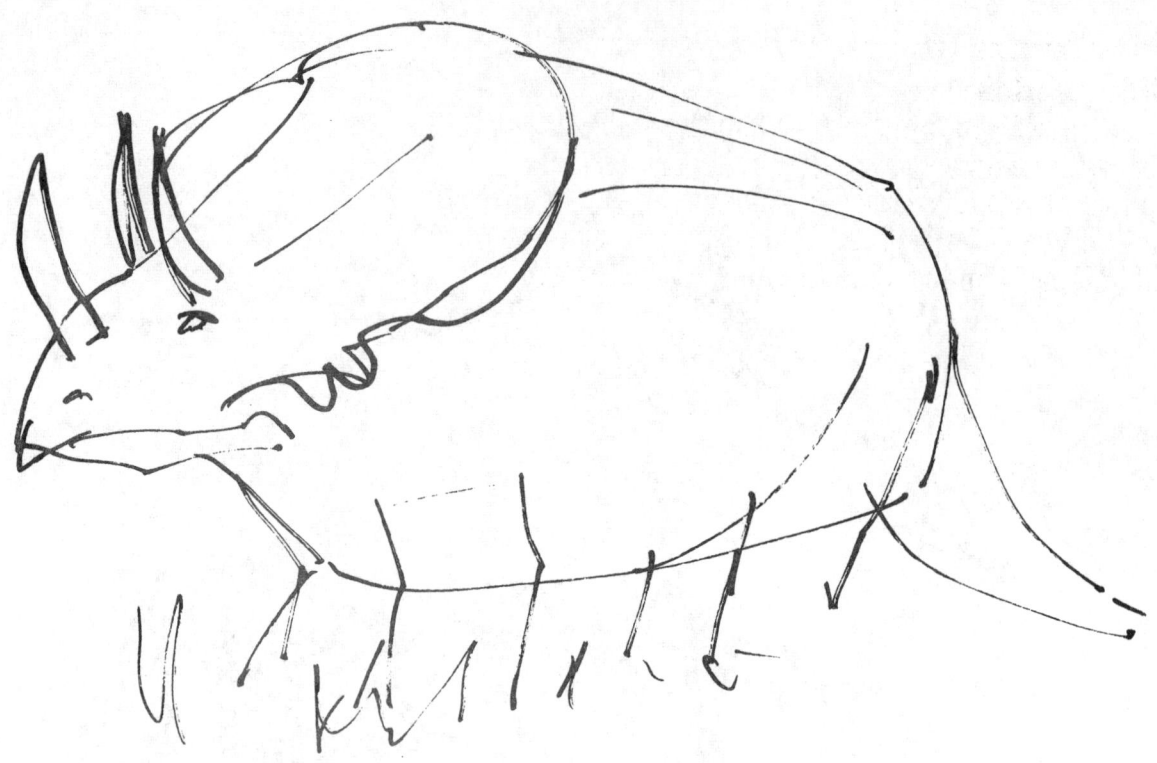

Triceratops – the king of the horned dinosaurs. It was about 6 metres (20 feet) long.

Pteranodon
– swift in flight, but awkward on the ground because of its weak legs. Probably a warm-blooded creature in spite of the fact it was a reptile.
Wingspan 8 metres (25 feet).

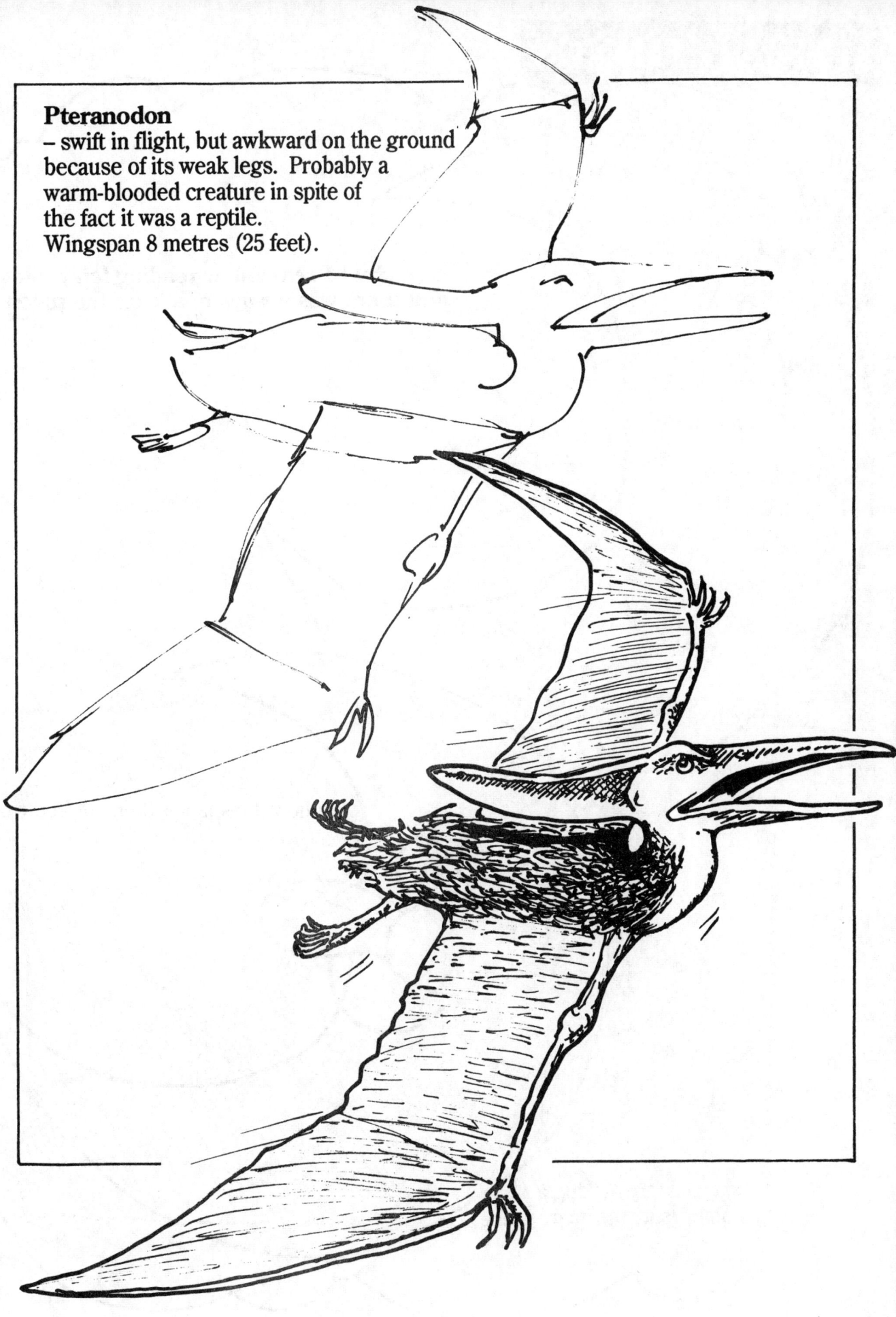

MAKING THINGS

As a child I remember reading fairy tales and there was always a face on the moon.

Follow the shapes, then put in the details.

You could try making a mobile using the moon shape.

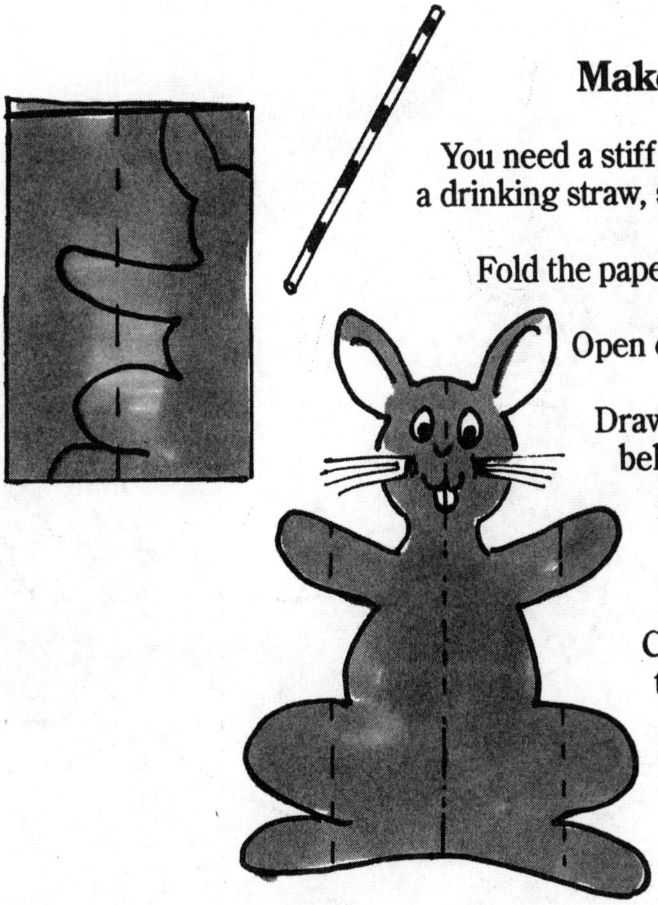

Make a paper bunny.

You need a stiff sheet of paper, a felt-tipped pen, a drinking straw, scissors and glue.

Fold the paper lengthwise, then fold it again in half.

Open out the paper so it's only folded once.

Draw the shape of the half bunny as shown below.

Cut out the rabbit shape, then use the pen to draw the features.

Cut whiskers from the straw and glue them onto the cheeks.

The rabbit should now freestand.

Try making different animals.

Silhouette pictures and portraits

Silhouette pictures can be very effective.
They can look extremely attractive framed.
Here you can see Harry Hedgehog,
Bently Badger, and Renny Fox out for a walk.
The long-eared owl is sitting on a branch.

Silhouette portraits

What you
need is paper
and a table lamp
(or torch). Pin the paper
on the wall. Get the person you
are going to draw to sit beside the lamp.
Sit between the lamp and the paper, so the light of
the lamp throws the shadow of the sitter on to the paper.
Draw around the outline, then paint the inside black.

Or stick paper or black card on paper, then cut around the line. This will give the
black silhouette, then you can stick the cut-out head back onto white paper. It can be great fun.

Here is another silhouette picture, this time a witch in flight.

Make a silhouette 'peep-show' theatre

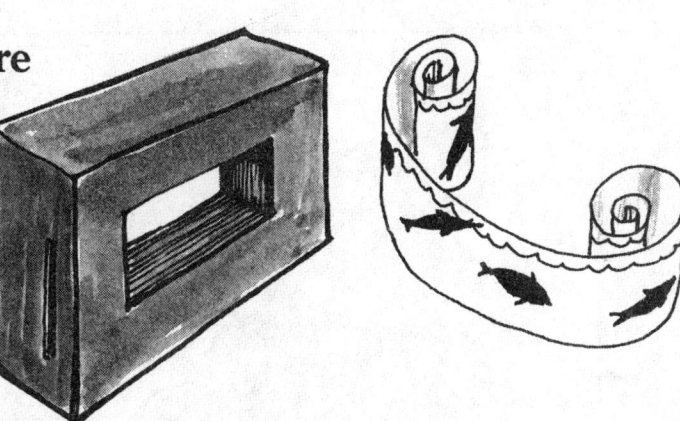

You need a small shoe box, scissors, a long strip of white paper with black silhouette cut-out shapes on it, a table lamp or torch.

Cut out a hole in the bottom and sides of the box as shown. Slide the paper through the slits.

Hint: make sure they are slightly bigger to help you move the paper easily through.

Place the box near the lamp and slide the paper through, telling your story to the audience.

73

TREES

This is to show you can turn almost anything into a cartoon character.

Oak trees chatting.

Pine trees windswept.

STORMY LAST NIGHT

CHRISTMAS

Why not try making your very own Christmas cards?
Jolly Santa seems a little stuck in the chimney.

Here is a standard type of snowman.

CHRISTMAS OWL

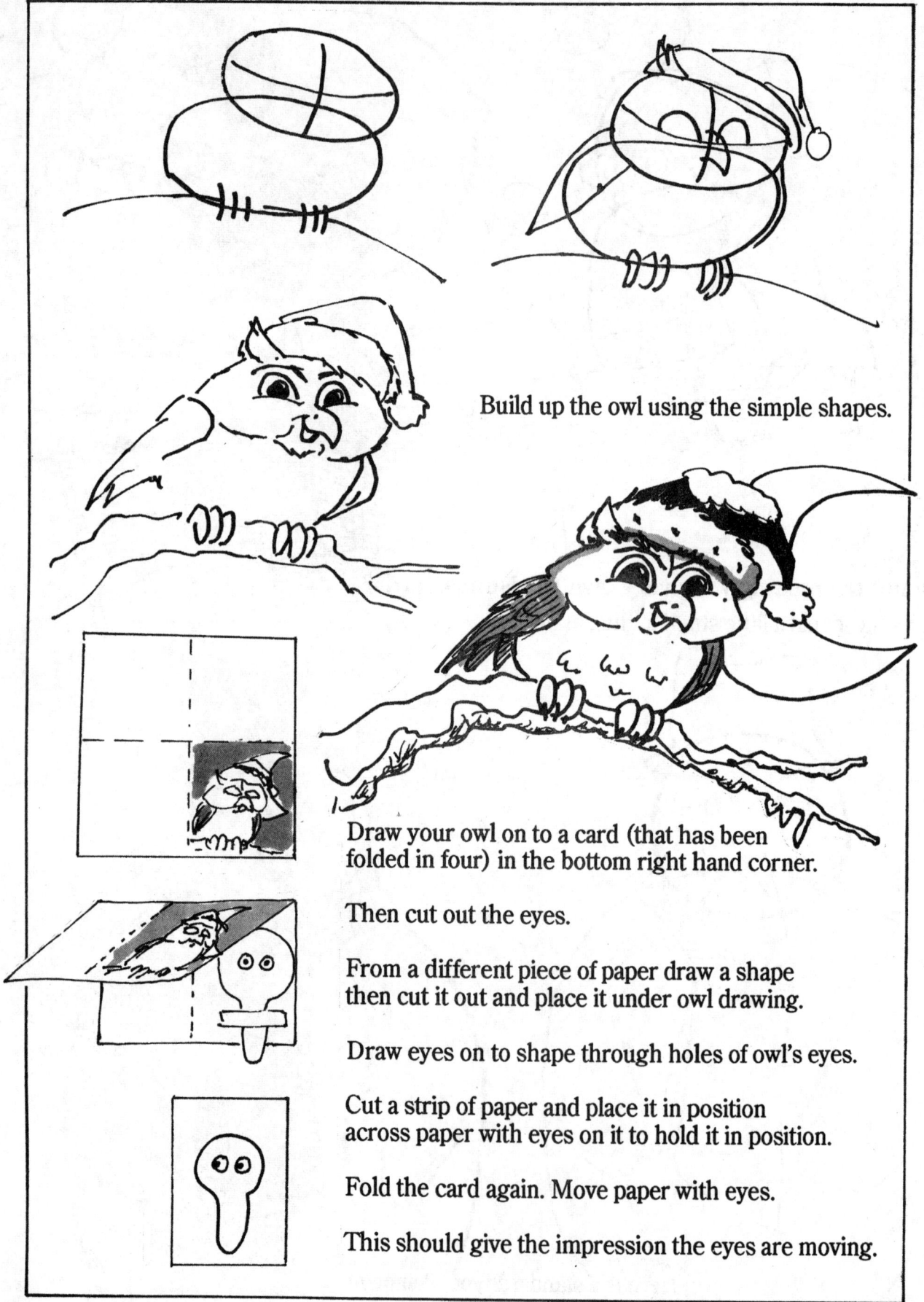

Build up the owl using the simple shapes.

Draw your owl on to a card (that has been folded in four) in the bottom right hand corner.

Then cut out the eyes.

From a different piece of paper draw a shape then cut it out and place it under owl drawing.

Draw eyes on to shape through holes of owl's eyes.

Cut a strip of paper and place it in position across paper with eyes on it to hold it in position.

Fold the card again. Move paper with eyes.

This should give the impression the eyes are moving.

More Santas to draw.

SCARY THINGS

MONSTERS

EGYPTIAN MUMMY

Start off with a very rough sketch to get movement and gesture.

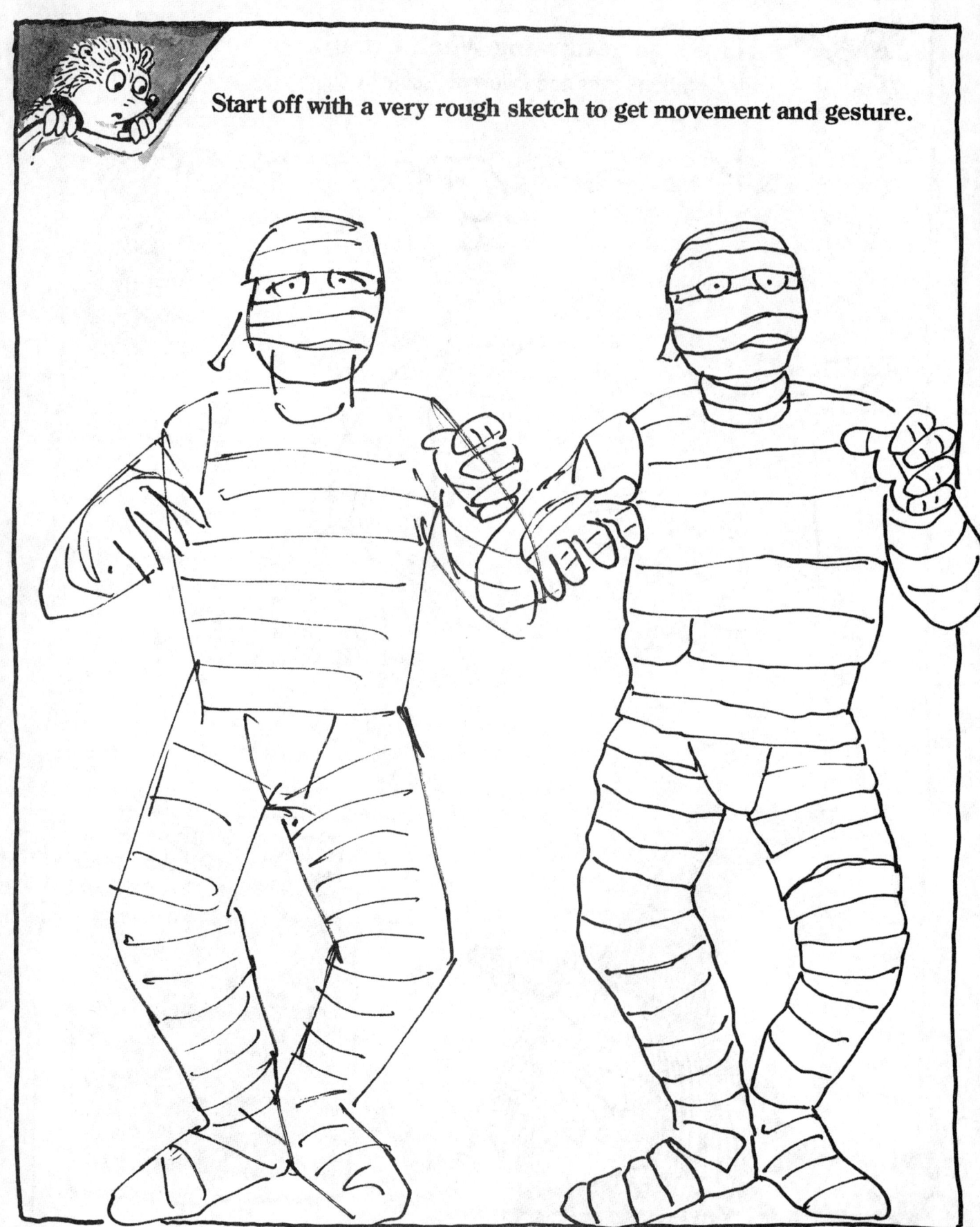

Using tone can give the figure a three-dimensional effect.

Hollywood has used the Egyptian mummy in many a horror movie to scare an audience.

FRANKENSTEIN'S MONSTER

DRACULA

Meet Count Dracula

Bram Stoker was responsible for him, and for many a sleepless night for me!
Where's the garlic?

GHOSTS

Here are a few ghosts to get you into the spirit of things!

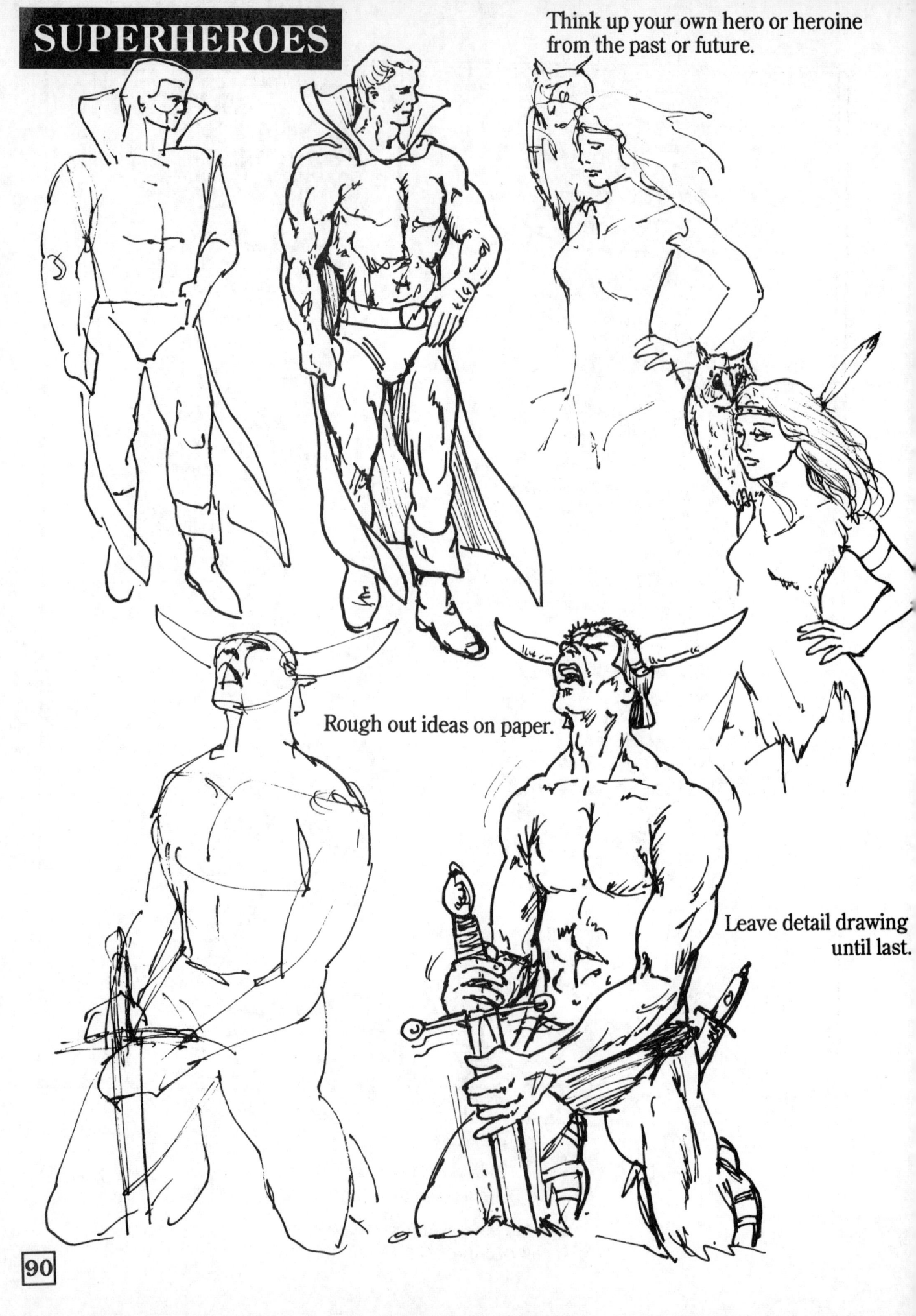

ACTION FIGURES

Using this rough skeleton
form you can work out the figure's pose.

Action figures are built up
on curved lines and movement.

You will soon learn to express the action,
which is more important than accuracy.

CARICATURES

William Shakespeare in his study thinking up his characters.
This caricature was done with a very fine-pointed pen.

Caricatures are funny drawings of real people.
Caricatures can be fun, but difficult to do.
What you have to do is exaggerate features, but keep it simple.

People with outstanding features are easier, e.g. a long nose, big ears, bulging eyes.
Study the face well before you begin.
Photos may help you.
Caricature your friends and family.

Other books by Don Conroy

Wings Series:
On Silent Wings
Wild Wings
Sky Wings

Tales of Woodlore Series:

The Owl Who Couldn't Hoot
The Tiger Who Was a Roaring Success
The Bat Who Was All in a Flap
The Hedgehog's Prickly Problem

The Celestial Child

All of these books will be re-issued in new formats during 1994 by The O'Brien Press.